DO IT *for* YOUR *future* SELF

Love you to the moon and back

for what is thoug
to be best in any re
point of view.
Motivation
the reason for he
purpose and di
act of motivatin
hat is thou

CAN'T
CAN

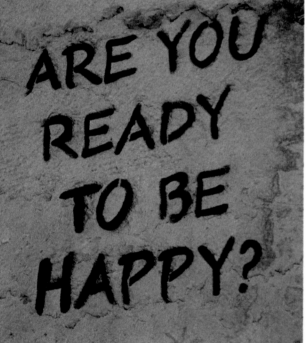

THINK
ABOUT
THINGS
DIFFERENTLY

ALL WE
HAVE
IS NOW

PUSH
HARDER
THAN
YESTERDAY

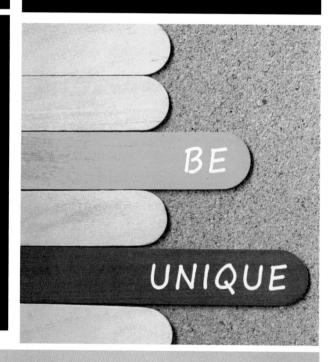

BE

UNIQUE

THINK
DECIDE
COMMIT
FOCUS
SUCCEED

DECIDE
COMMIT
FOCUS
SUCCEED

Made in the USA
Las Vegas, NV
27 December 2023

83555917R00031